Sez She
To Me

John Pepper

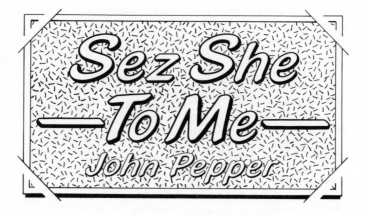

Sez She To Me

John Pepper

Illustrations by Ralph Dobson

Appletree Press

for Barbara and Hilary

First published and printed by
The Appletree Press Ltd
7 James Street South
Belfast BT2 8DL
1984

British Library Cataloguing in Publication Data
Pepper, John
 Sez she to me.
 1. English language—Dialects—Northern Ireland
 I. Title
 427′.9416   PE2586

ISBN 0-86281-139-2

Contents

Preface

The women of Ulster speak in these pages. The speakers have been selected not so much for what they said, or for their profundity, rather for the way they said it, and their lively and caustic use of the English language.

Here are placed on record women's effusions when shopping ('Them roses are that real lookin' you'd think they were artificial'), gossiping, chatting in the bus, talking to the woman next door, waiting in a supermarket queue, or exasperated by a husband ('Steak's far too dear for an oul lad who only lies in bed and plays bowls').

I am convinced that the examples I have affectionately chronicled bring the speaker more vividly to life than if in each case it was specified that she was plump, thin, peevish, greying, blonde, or had a cabbage patch face. If the syntax is often ruptured the liveliness survives.

And if the members of my own sex are largely by-passed my aim has been to stress the unique quality of the observations chosen (like that made by the woman at her husband's wake: 'He was worse many a time than the time he died'). I do not seek to demonstrate whether or not a woman's tongue is the sharper or the more penetrating.

The examples have come to me from many sources. To all of them I am genuinely grateful.

John Pepper

Hands like a feather duster

Who is most likely to have exclaimed, 'He's the kind of man you have to take the right way—by the throat'?

Who is most liable to have made the complaint, 'It hasn't stopped raining since it started'?

Who runs a fair chance of having declared, 'The look that woman gives you is like a poultice of hot cinders'?

And who in all probability grumbled, 'I'm all behind this morning'?

Were I to say that the answer in every case is a lady, I would be cracked, to use the Ulster idiom. Each help to underline the message that the feminine contribution to the zest of everyday speech in Ulster is more formidable than the ladies are given credit for. When it comes from a woman's lips the overheard comment will often be more colourful, more caustic and more quotable than if it were a male utterance. This is incontrovertible.

W.C. Fields said, 'A woman drove me to drink and I never even thanked her.' A debt is certainly owed to the ladies for their lavish donations to the examples of lively utterance which come my way.

'She was the colour of a livin' corpse,' is infinitely more expressive than 'She wasn't looking well.' 'A coat's a right hap on a freezin' day' is unquestionably more graphic than 'Cold, isn't it?'

Paying its own tribute to a physician with a delicate

9

'He has hands like a feather duster.'

touch is the statement, 'I haven't a word to say about that new doctor at the health clinic. He has hands like a feather duster.'

During a Royal visit an Ulsterwoman was heard exclaiming delightedly, 'Look, the Queen's wearing my shoes!' She could not have chosen a neater way to draw attention to the fact that her footwear matched Her Majesty's.

It is safe to say that scenic delights are not the only attractions Northern Ireland offers the visitor. The womenfolk can be relied on to say a mouthful almost every time they speak, as was the case with the mother watching her children paddling in the sea on a windy afternoon: 'I'm dead scared of them bein' cowped by one of them title waves. I'd be beside myself.'

'You could tell she was well brought up by the way she always rifts behine her hand,' shows an enthusiasm for the niceties of social behaviour. It is important to know that the lady was troubled with 'the wind' and did all she could to conceal it.

A woman driver was told by the indignant pedestrian she had managed to nudge aside, 'You should be locked up, you bline ijit', bringing the retort, 'I hit you, didn't I?' And a revelation which speaks for itself was, 'Sez she to me I hev hailstones and I don't know how I'm going to be able to weather them.'

There was also a distinctive touch about the remark to an election candidate, 'You must be sick, sore and tired of shaking hands with so many strange faces.'

A pair of wearin' trousers

If anything is guaranteed to turn an Ulsterwoman on it is shopping. It brings out the best—and the worst—in them, I have found.

One went into a drapery store carrying a kitchen mop. She told the assistant, 'I'm lookin' for curtains for the back bedroom. Blue ones.' Then she held the mop aloft and added, 'This is the length of them. It's dead on.'

Another lady on the same quest produced two pieces of string and explained, 'The short one is the wideness and this one is the length, and don't forget to throw in an extra piece for the pelvis.'

In a busy supermarket a shopper was asked by a complete stranger, 'Could you tell me where I could find a rubbish bin?' She was told obligingly, 'Look, I'll take you. I'm going that way myself as a matter of fact.' When the hardware section was reached the assistant was told, 'This lady wants a rubbish bin.' One was soon produced but before the assistant could explain, 'This is the only kind we have in stock', the stranger brought the skin of a banana from her pocket, dropped it in, said 'Thanks very much' and walked off.

Another example of a classic misunderstanding occurred when a shopper said to another stranger 'Could you help me? I'm in need of a pulley.' She was directed to the Ladies.

A woman was examining with her husband a display of

blankets and was pounced on by an eager salesman, bubbling with sales talk. 'You're looking awfully well, madam. Isn't the weather quite cool? Still a shade cold, though? Cold enough for a good pair of blankets, eh? You're sure to be interested in this special offer. The value we have in these blankets is astonishing.' Drily came the comment, 'Howl yer tongue, man. We have far better value in them at home. Don't we, John?'

'A pair of wearin' trousers for my husband,' was one request. 'The last pair he got here were a lovely fit but they were far too long in the length.'

It is not unusual to hear the lament, 'I bought the wee lad a new pullover last week and I'll swear to me God he'll be through the elbows of it before he has it right on.'

After buying some cocktail sausages in a corner shop a woman asked, 'Have you any sticks?' 'Sorry,' came the reply, 'but we've nothing but firelighters.'

In one establishment a woman explained that her husband had mislaid his gloves while walking around with her and waited while a search was made. Before long a girl assistant came up, placed a pair on the counter, and said, 'Them them?' Fowler probably turned in his grave.

I have heard the request being made for, 'Half a pound of that cheese—the one with the blue rinse.'

A woman who asked in a North Antrim shop for a half a pound of biscuits added, 'No broken ones, please.' She was immediately challenged 'Are you going to ate them hale, then?'

In a chemist's a customer was heard telling a friend, 'The woman next door kep' goin' on about her migrane and I said she should try yoga. I ran into her a week after and asked her how she was gettin' on with it. Sez she to me, "It didn't agree with me at all. It kep' repeatin' on me".'

A sore plaster

Whether Ulster-English presents more difficulties to the uninitiated than Scouse-English, Geordie-English, Tyke-English or any other linguistic variation is a nice question. There would be complications in translating for the benefit of a Greek shopkeeper with a scanty knowledge of English what a customer meant when she pointed to his over-ripe bananas and said, 'If you don't get rid of them soon they'll be going.'

A similar problem would arise if he were to be told, 'My Geordie's a right plaster. That's why we didden bring him this time.' Geordie would also qualify for the label 'a sore plaster' yet if his wife heard anyone else call him one it would bring a torrent of abuse.

The holidaymaker who said, 'After a fortnight in mutton dummies it won't be easy startin' to speak English again' would baffle a good many listeners unaware that this was a reference to gutties, or sneakers.

'It's so hot I think we should have our dinner outside,' a hotel guest said to her husband. A German sitting near nodded and murmured, 'Warm nicht.' The woman turned to him and said delightedly, 'Goodness, I never took you for being Scattish. I was sure you were one of them oul Germans.' Eagerly her husband joined in, 'I took you for a kraut as well.'

In a Spanish resort a Belfast girl, invited to go skin

'The wee lad came home ringin'.'

diving, excused herself by saying, 'I have no head for depths.' And translating for the benefit of a native of Marbella what was meant by the statement, 'The wee lad came home ringin'' has certain difficulties.

Continental traders in their encounters with shoppers from Ulster must often give up in despair. How are they to know that 'She's all right' can indicate (a) 'She's a decent wee woman', (b) 'She has a heart of corn', (c) 'I wouldn't really like to trust her', (d) 'I could take her or leave her'? All it is often meant to convey is that the lady has got over a bout of illness.

The Portuguese porter who was asked, 'Wud ye take thon beg out forrus?' would probably have a fair idea what was meant if the speaker pointed at the luggage. This would not be the case if the man wanted to know the time and was told, 'I'm not sure but it's gettin' on.'

Shopping abroad is far from being child's play for the trader. 'Could I try on a left-hand shoe?' could make for some confusion as would, 'I'm luckin' a perra black shoes, big size savan, way a wee heel and not too dear. They're onny for a bicycle.'

Certainly it is hard to come by an appropriate reply to, 'In this hate them frozen goods of yours must go like hot cakes.'

The cups
I was married in

It is wise to be wary of an offer of hospitality in Northern Ireland. Visitors should note that the information, 'You'll only be gettin' a mouthful in your hand but it'll keep the heart in you till the table's set,' does not imply that the table has to be shifted to a special position, just that it won't be laid.

The woman who said, 'Aunt Nelly just loves a cup of tea out' merely meant that Nelly felt that tea in a café was hard to beat.

When a guest praised her hostess's tea-set it brought the reply, 'Aye, they're all right. They're the cups I was married in.' Her humble upbringing was reflected in the confession, 'I'm dyin' about a cup in a bowel.' However, it should be said that the popularity in country areas of a bowl of tea is dying out.

A group of Ulster holidaymakers left a landlady in an English resort quite bewildered when she asked if they would like tea that evening and was told, 'Yes, but we'll just take if for the drink.'

If it is said of a husband 'He can't get enough parge', it shows he has a fondness for porridge at breakfast. It is a safe guess that he prefers it thick, which his small son would describe as, 'The kind that says "puff, puff, puff" and not "clip, clap, clip, clap" when it's boilin'.'

A Belfast parent whose son embarrassed her by upsetting

a full glass of orange juice over the newly covered table in a Spanish hotel had the waitress guessing by explaining, 'You could take him nowhere so you could.'

The invitation, 'Come round in an hour. You needn't bother dressin' for you'll just be gettin' a slice of apple tart on your knee,' should not be taken literally. A plate is certain to be provided.

If it should be said of an ailing husband, 'He's on the mend for he ast for the pan before I was up out of my bed this mornin'' he is clearly a man 'never behind the door when there's a good pan'.

A County Down woman who arrived for a short stay with her sister-in-law explained as she unpacked, 'I'm stupid. I've been and gone and forgot my slippers. Would it be all right if I had the lend of yours? I just want to make a cup of tea in them.' It is not unlikely that she was related to the woman who confided 'I was late gettin' home last night and when I got in there was yer man making cocoa in his socks.'

Ulsterwomen are generous to a fault. At the drop of a hat you'll be invited to 'Come over the marra for a wee bit of lunch. I'm not much of a cook I know but I'll throw you up somethin'.'

Care should be taken in voicing appreciation. The guest who said, 'I always say there's nathin like a piece of home-made cake no matter how bad it is' bit her lip too late. Then she asked, 'Is this your Christmas cake?' and was told 'No, it's just our through-the-week cake.' After that all was well.

To complain, 'She never even asked me had I a mouth on me' applies in those cases where a 'giving hand' is conspicuously absent. This is also the case when the comment is heard, 'I was left standing with my two arms the one length.'

He lies in his bed and plays bowls

Special considerations come into play for the man of whom it was said, 'Steak's too dear for an oul lad that does nathan but lie in his bed and play bowls till he's blue in the face.'

In a Shankill Road bus a woman who was asked how she was keeping replied, 'Me? I'm sufferin' from retired husband, so I am. I'm kilt makin' him parge in the mornin', Bovril at alavan, peelin' spuds for his dinner at one. Then there's biled egg an' scraped toast for his tay and anor cuppa tay with piles of sugar before he goes till his bed. I'm wore out so I am.'

Appreciation for an evening out is obvious in the comment, 'He took me to see a play and it was a roar. I'm not tellin' you a word of a lie. He laughed his head aff and I hadn't an eye to see out aff. Everybody was in stitches. You should go an' see it yourself for you'll split your sides. There wasn't a dry eye in the place. The woman sittin' beside me—I'm sure she wet herself.'

Other husbands sometimes come in for high praise, as in, 'He's a tidy wee man. He would never pass you.' His credentials were securely established by his nod of recognition. Forget the nod and you're the worst in the world.

Another encounter did not create quite the same warmth. 'We had a nice wee chat for he seemed to be a plite wee sort of a man. Then he said, "Cheerio then, I'll be on my way. I'll knock you up some time."' There was a pause before it

19

'Steak's too dear for an oul lad that does nathan but lie there in his bed and play bowls.'

was added, 'That's when he was near gettin' a slap up the bake.'

It was said of one husband, 'Sure he's away out for a game of indoor bowls.' Of another it was explained, 'You'll not fine him in the day an' forby he starts nights in the mornin'.'

An interesting domestic revelation was, 'I said to our Jimmy in bed last night that I was goin' to wash me hair but I just thought I wouldn't bother me head. He said I was just right. He's a wee balla fire.'

Another marital disclosure ran, 'He's gat hisself a wee bit of a job, thank God. The wages is ridiculus but the money's not bad.'

An elderly couple were selling their house and, as usual, the wife was showing a prospective buyer round. 'This is our lounge', she said proudly. Her husband, reading a newspaper by the fireside, looked up and exclaimed, 'Dear me. I've been livin' here for twenty years and I never knew before we had a lounge.'

It takes years of married life to avoid misunderstandings. A Toronto lady, married just over a year there to a Ballymena man, was taken out for dinner and at the end of the meal he said, 'Have you a pain?' She assumed that he felt she wasn't showing a proper appreciation of the meal and rather snapped back, 'Of course I haven't.' Just then the waiter came up and the husband said to him, 'Have *you* a pain?' Instantly a Biro was produced and the husband used it to sign the bill. The wife realised with embarrassment that the waiter knew the Ballymena way of putting things better than she did.

The cat's eatin' like a horse

As a rule women become more attached to a pet than most men, although it may be argued that women don't go overboard about pigeons to the same extent as their husbands.

The lady who was told, 'That's not a bad wee dog you have' and instantly retorted, 'He's not meant to be a bad wee dog', made her point. So did the woman who was asked the breed of the dog she had on a lead and said, 'All I know is it isn't an Asslation for I wouldn't have one of them big slabbery brutes about the place.'

In another case a woman was advised, 'With all this kidnapping that's going on you should be careful about taking your wee Bimbo for a walk at night.' The advice was taken calmly. 'Who would want to kidnap the like of wee Bimbo?' she demanded. 'Sure they would drap us at the nearest lamp they came to and that would suit wee Bimbo down to the groun'.'

This assessment of a holiday boarding house was probably pretty accurate: 'It says "no dogs" so we won't bother. I don't like them boardin' houses where if you miss your dinner you've had it.'

The anguish of the lady on the beach who was desperately trying to get her dog to leave the water led her to utter the ultimate in threats: 'If you don't come back out this minute I'll not bring you here again.'

A baffled pet owner summed up her frustration in the

words, 'I took the wee dog out for a walk and when I got her home she was throwing rings round her, yet the only shop we were in was the jeweller's.'

Another walk that ended in disappointment was put into this form: 'I thought I'd take the wee pet to the Giant's Causeway but we didn't like it one bit. It was terrible stoney.'

One pet owner was devoted to a rather crafty mongrel which could scratch at the door with its paws when it wanted into the house. One evening she was annoyed at having to leave her favourite television programme to open the door for it. As she was doing so an army patrol was passing and one of the soldiers who had been watching the dog with interest said, 'That's a smart wee animal you have there, missus.' In a flash came her response, 'Smart? Sure that's the second time this week he's forgot his key.'

While the chihuahua is a popular pet among the ladies the budgerigar runs it close. One owner was heard to tell a friend, 'A woman I know, sez she to me, the best thing I could do was to get the wee chiguana sprayed by a vit. What do you think I should do?'

Another cry of distress was, 'The poor wee budgie has been diseased for the last twelve months and more. It used to be able to fly roun' the house like a bird.' Then she added, 'It just fell down dead at my feet and do you know this? It has had me annoyed ever since.'

In a different category was the woman who insisted, 'The cat must be goin' to have kittens. It's eatin' like a horse. Ye cudden be up to them.'

That dog's a wee marvel

A marked change has taken place in the status of man's best friend (or should it be a person's best friend?) with dog wardens now everywhere on the prowl following legislation to curb strays. It is true that the warden in one town quit after only a few weeks in office, complaining that he had been hounded out of his job by angry pet owners. Nevertheless, the general attitude to the possession of a pooch remains doggedly dedicated.

A dog in the eyes of her mistress can acquire almost human characteristics, as happened with the Highland terrier a woman in a park stopped to admire. 'See that wee dog,' the owner told her with pride, 'she knows every word I say, every move I make. A wee marvel. She heard that much talk about the licence going up to £5 that she thought I wouldn't be keeping her. You could see she was worried sick. Just went to scrapins. But from the day and hour I paid the £5 she started mending and there's been no holding her back ever since.'

A collie's lack of appetite bothered another owner so much that a friend was consulted. 'Why not let me have it for a couple or days and I'll cure it for you?' the friend suggested. The man was as good as his word and when the dog was returned it was completely back to normal. 'What on earth did you do?' the friend was asked. 'It was easy. I shut him up in our roof space for the last three days and gave him nothing but water.'

'She knows every word I say, every move I make. A wee marvel.'

Quite exceptional qualities were credited to a Labrador owned by a devoted churchgoer. 'The last minister we had,' she explained, 'was a great believer in short sermons and the dog would always sit waiting for me outside the church to go home with me. But the new man we have now is awful long-winded. You couldn't shut him up, and lo and behold the dog won't budge now when I try to bring him to church. He just stays at home. Boys, but they can be the wise animals.'

An equally enthusiastic claim was made for a springer. 'A walkin' wonder. I've never seen his like. I've sold him five times and he always comes back.'

A County Down farmer's wife, indignant that her husband should have acquired a second dog without consulting her, roared, 'That's two we've got now. Sure you know right well we haven't barkin' for two dogs.' It was an attitude at variance with that of the woman who asked a shopkeeper, 'Could you recommend some biscuits that would do this wee dog of mine. He's twelve and he's on his last legs. He's my wee friend.' But there was nothing sentimental about the comment which followed the news that a neighbour had come into a small legacy: 'If I know her she'll be doing her messages with a poodle before you know.'

He said a burial got him out

It is constantly insisted that 'the wake is passing' but the deep-rooted nature of the custom, based on the philosophy that life goes on, is marked by the Belfast comment, 'Yon woman's the sort that would spoil a good wake.' It provides an occasion to reflect on the inevitable. It is not strictly an opportunity to be melancholy.

As a guest stood solemnly beside the coffin at a County Antrim wake he was told encouragingly, 'If he was half at himself this night he would be right and glad to see you.'

Of a Fermanagh handyman, said to have been the victim of 'a sudden claps' a woman friend said, 'He wasn't a bad cratur. He would have done you a good turn if he was able. Many a time he put a neighbour's windy in that somebody broke. Luck at him. You'd swear he nodded his head that it wasn't a word of a lie.'

A tribute which brought murmurs of warm approval was, 'Although he wasn't all that healthy himself he wore out a good bit of shoe leather trampin' to the funerals of the healthy ones. He was awful fond of a burial. He always said it got him out. I'm glad to see he has his walkin' boots on him.'

Asides overheard at wakes show that the convention of 'never speaking ill of the dead' is not always observed. 'I would never have it said that I would speak of anybody that's passed away but if you listened to some people they'd tell you that he borrowed money and never paid it back. Even if it isn't true it's not for me to say.'

'So he's away at last,' a mourner murmured. 'He was a brave kindly wee man with a heart of corn. He'd never harm a fly.' Then she added in more subdued tones, 'To tell you the truth he was that mean he'd have skinned a flea for its hide.'

If it is said, 'The crack at John's wake was grand', it is no less a tribute to John than to his widow. One who sat inconsolable beside her husband's coffin was scolded by a neighbour, 'For goodness sake, Maggie, quit yer girnin'. Sure you won't be long after him.'

A bereaved wife said of her loss 'To be honest I'll no be sorry to go myself for he's been in that bed of his for an awful long time. It'll be a relief when my turn comes and I'll be resting in Beelzebub's bosom myself.' Quietly the minister corrected her, 'You must mean Abraham's, don't you?' 'Maybe,' she answered, 'but if you had been in my shoes as long as me you wouldn't be a bit particular about his name.'

At a County Tyrone wake it was said of a deceased farmhand, 'It'll be a relief for him to be gone for he had a cough that would wreck a row of houses.' This brought the reply, 'Maybe so, but there's many a one in the graveyard that would be proud and glad to have it this minute.'

A widow who was left rather more money than she expected told her friends, 'There was a bit more than I thought there'd be so I bought him a good coffin. I said to myself that it wouldn't be wasted. Sure it'll last him a lifetime.'

Tactfulness is not always conspicious on these occasions. 'You know that verse she had in the paper about him? "His willing hands will toil no more." Woman dear, the sowl hasn't done a hand's turn if he could help it this many a year.'

I want
to be crematarted

Choice of a last resting place is generally considered a matter of grave importance, they say in North Antrim.

This was made clear by the woman who told a friend, 'We went for a walk through the new cemetery. It was that nice, I thought to myself, but I wouldn't like to be buried there. I'd rather go to the old cemetery. That's where all my oul friends are buried and I'd feel far more at home.'

A sentiment on the same lines was voiced by the lady whose husband had taken the precaution of buying a grave on a cemetery hill: 'If we're spared we'll have a lovely view.'

A graveyard visitor expressed a not dissimilar opinion. 'I wouldn't mind one bit being laid to rest out here. It's that nice and healthy, away from all the smoke and the smell of petrol from the traffic.'

One woman was particularly explicit. 'When I die I want to be crematarted.' She was asked, 'Don't you mean cremated?' She retorted, 'Whatever it is I'd rather have it than be buried.'

A Belfastwoman explained to a friend, 'I went to the City Hall to make the arrangements for a grave for Charley, then I went to the cemetery to give the man there the number. "You've picked a good dry spot," he told me. I thought it was terrible nice of the man.'

After a funeral a mourner commented, 'It was terrible. When we got there we found there was a strike of grave-

'If we're spared we'll have a lovely view.'

diggers. You've no idea what it was like. All them funerals and not a gravedigger in sight. Then a minister came up and was very angry. He kicked up the devil and got them all buried—every one of them.' She nodded in wonder at the miracle.

'I want a card for a man who has just died,' a woman said breathlessly in a stationery shop just as it was about to close. 'I beg your pardon,' said the puzzled shopkeeper. 'A card. A card,' repeated the woman impatiently. 'You mean a sympathy card, do you?' she was asked. 'Ach, I suppose that'll do rightly,' was her reply.

Bereavement brings special complications. A photographer was asked to take a picture of the deceased as he lay in his coffin. For some reason he was still wearing his hat and she asked specifically that he should be taken with his hat off. 'No trouble,' said the photographer, 'but can you tell me what way he parted his hair? I'm sure you'll want to have it as lifelike as possible.' 'Ach,' he was assured, 'you'll see when he takes his hat off, won't you?'

Ulster hospital staffs are warned to be careful about what they say when giving information to inquirers about a patient who has been discharged. They are enjoined on no account to say to a caller, 'She's away.' 'She went two hours ago,' is also taboo. Either of these can be taken to imply the worst.

A new tenant on a postman's round handed him back a letter addressed to the former tenant, saying, 'He's gone.' 'Where to?' he asked. 'That depends on the life he led,' she answered. 'He's dead.'

The simple statement, 'I had an aunt buried yesterday by marriage,' could be put differently. So often it isn't, just because it is understood.

Have you the crack time?

Anyone who is stopped in a Belfast street and is asked, 'Have you the crack time?' should not get the idea that 'a bit of your crack' is being invited. What is sought is Greenwich Mean Time. Sometimes it can be 'the right time'. It is all because of the underlying suspicion harboured by many that most people have cheap, unreliable timepieces, not usually to be trusted.

Of course there is the more direct and more trusting 'Have you the time?' There is also the flattering 'How much time have you?' when the inquiry comes from an attractive member of the opposite sex after you have been introduced.

'Isn't it late?' has a challenge of its own, and the reply liable to come from someone without a watch is, 'I'm not actually sure but it's rightly on.' This can throw the stranger. It can mean that it isn't far off lunch-time. In mid-afternoon it can indicate that it is close on six. Around ten o'clock in the evening it shows it is getting on for midnight. You take your choice. It all reflects the Ulster lack of hesitation about calling on a stranger for help.

There is a constant urge to consult the passer-by with a confidence that the odds are against a dusty answer. It reflects the extent to which the Province still has a small-town attitude, a feeling that on the whole people are friendly, and won't turn you away. But this assurance is put to the test when, as happened less than fifty yards from Belfast's famous Albert Clock, a woman with a baby in her arms accosted a younger woman and said, 'Excuse me, but do you know the time?'

Appeals to passers-by are not confined to the time of day. You can be stopped and asked if you know a good place to get signwriter's brushes, or a pair of navy blue gloves, or the way to a shop that sells letter openers.

One woman was asked, 'Do you know the best place to get some black crêpe for the widow next door?' A day's collection of one elderly lady, all from complete strangers, consisted of, 'Where could I get some weed killer for our lettuces?' 'You wouldn't know a Mrs McQuilt who lives in a corner house near Botanic Gardens?', and, 'Would you happen to know if McCrudden's pub is still in the same place?'

There are occasions when a confession of ignorance can be greeted with deep suspicion, as if you know perfectly well but are stubbornly holding the information back. This only happens when desperation has set in. Often an inquiry is an excuse for a harmless chat, an innocent display of friendliness in an alien world. 'Would you happen to know a shop that sells leather elbow patches?' or 'Excuse me, mister, but do you think it'll turn to rain?' can often signal loneliness, a desire to talk to somebody—anybody.

Only the most churlish will give a brusque, impatient answer to a stranger's question. It can open up all kinds of possibilities to be asked, 'Is the Clock Bar near here?' and to reply at once, 'You buyin'?'

There are times when tact is needed, as was the case with the woman in a furniture store who was studying a bedroom suite with her husband. 'You can buy them in bits, can't you?' she asked the salesman, who could only respond with a wry nod.

I sat up downstairs all night

Ulster people home after a long absence will know they are back on their native soil even if they go around with their eyes shut. The voices that fill the air, rather than the familiar landmarks, are all they need.

After a five year absence in Canada an Ulsterwoman knew she was home when she asked a friend how she was, and was told, 'Ach, I'm not so good. In fact I sat up downstairs all last night so I did.'

The comment made as a group of members of a women's organisation was about to set off on a bus outing could not have been heard anywhere else. They waited for one member about whom there was some doubt whether her husband would allow her to go. Then someone exclaimed, 'Ah, he's let her go. There she is. I can see she has on her.'

The statement, 'When I see that man I wouldn't look at him', is a typically native way of indicating lack of regard, as in, 'He's not up to much.' This also applies to 'He'd remind you of a fella that would lift a feather with a duck at the end of it', if the speaker comes from the country rather than the town.

Often the style in which a criticism is made can show considerable diplomatic delicacy. At the funeral of a widow it was said that a distant relative, without consulting any of the others, had generously made arrangements to send her only daughter to a boarding school. Yet this produced the comment, 'That was very forward of him.' What was meant was that he had a hell of a nerve.

Rather more forthright was the reply of the woman who was asked, 'Does your man like pizzazzas?' 'Them?' she answered. 'He'll ate anything set in front of him that isn't nailed down.'

Boxing tournament audiences are not always confined to the male sex. Feminine criticisms of poor contests can be as deflating as that made by the men. Of one middle-weight encounter a woman was heard telling her companion, 'Isn't this desperate, Jinny? Pure murder. Where do they get them? Them two cudden bate their way out of a paper beg. Many's the night me and the oul man put on a far better show than them two craters.'

The same quality of disapproval was shown by the criticism, 'That woman's trippin' over herself with consate. She can't even pass a shap winda without wavin' at herself.'

It takes a moment or two to grasp what was meant by the woman who thought her house had been overlooked in a door-to-door distribution of soap samples. She dashed after the girl distributor and complained. A sample was instantly handed over with apologies. On returning to the house the woman discovered that a sample had actually been left. It was found behind the door. She ran after the distributor to explain and offered the second sample back. 'Just you keep it, missus,' she was told. 'That's for bananst.'

An Ulsterwoman will see nothing wrong in making the request, 'Would you do me an awful favour?' and if she says, 'My man's working away', will be astonished if she has given the impression that his job is a long way from home.

We have our tea tuk

Dining out has elements of its own in Ulster. A shopping interlude over a cup of tea provides an excuse equalled only by a chat over the garden fence, at the corner of the street, or under a hair dryer.

Two women waiting to be served were discussing television repeats and one asked, 'Do you like Mickey Rooney?' 'I'd rather have spaghetti,' was the reply.

As she studied the menu a woman said to her companion, 'I think I'd fancy a beef burglar.' After a pause the reply came 'Right enough. I'd fancy a beef burglar myself.'

Two women were obviously enjoying their chat over tea, laughing a great deal, and not bothering about the cups. A waitress approached and asked, 'Is there anything else I can get you?', expecting an order for another pot. 'No daughter,' she was told. 'Sall right. We have our tea tuk.'

Every conceivable topic is covered over a café cup of tea:

The weather: 'Isn't there a quare drap in the nights?' Or, 'That hate's desprit. I'm swatin' the piece out. After this I'm after a pair of sunglasses for my head's jumpin'.

Husbands: 'Know what I'm goin' till tell ye? My man coughed all day there the other night.' 'My man came home well oiled, so he did. This mornin' he was rusty all right.'

Bereavement: As a widow sipped a cup of tea with a friend not long after the funeral: 'If only our Hughie had waited he could have had a cup of tea here with us, so he could. He was a quare man for a toasted scone.'

'They're fantastic for flickin'.'

Other women: 'Mrs McKinnick there, she's a cute one. Nathan but a big lump. There's nat much of another body's business that woman likes to miss.'

Relations: 'My brother's comin' home from Canada next week. I don't suppose I'll recognise him for he's been out there now for nearly forty years.' 'Then he won't be able to recognise you either.' 'Rubbitch, woman. Of course he will. Sure I haven't been away anywhere since he left.'

Youngsters: 'You'd take your end at the childer nowadays. I ast our wee Sammy what he thought of the school meals an' he said the beef curry wasn't bad so long as you're starvin'. I ast him if he liked the peas and he said, "They're great, ma. They're fantastic for flickin'.

Friends: 'Mrs McGurk's wee girl's got a job in the Post Office. Nice wee thing. I tole her you couldn't lick sellin' stamps for a steady job.'

One woman, as she carefully put her parcels on the floor beside her, announced: 'I'm dun. Them ones in the shaps these days—ye cudden be up to them. I was waitin' in the butcher's for my ribs and the man ast, "Who's next?" I said I was after the wee lad standin' beside me. He said, "Get away there, missus. Why doan you go after somebody your own age?" I tole him to catch himself on, that it was his ribs I was after.'

On top of my head
I had a bad stummick

Whether or not it is the climate, Ulsterwomen are prone to complain of 'a funny back', 'a funny knee', 'a funny stomach', 'a funny ankle', 'a funny head', or even 'a funny ear'. None of these afflictions can be said to be a cause for hilarity.

One lament ran, 'The wee girl took a funny leg and we couldn't get to the bottom of it. She went to do her messages in the bus.'

Another took the form of, 'I asked the chemist if he could give me something for my flatulence. He told me he couldn't but they sold repair kits in the bicycle shop next door.'

Stomachs are a constant source of anxiety. Few parts of the anatomy take the cake to such a remarkable degree. The lady of whom it was said, 'She's laid up with her stummick', explained, 'It has been as hard as a drum for the last three days. I was up the walls.' She could also have been 'down with her stummick' or just 'bad with it'.

To have a 'churnin' stummick' is not a condition to be envied. Usually the afflicted will gamely try to keep going. If a male stomach misbehaves this style of obstinacy is not usually in evidence.

'Why aren't you in your bed?' a woman was asked. She replied, 'I have a cowl on my stummick. I know rightly. But sure the weather wasn't too bad so I thought I'd take myself out to break myself in.' Another response to the same ques-

39

tion was, 'I have a shocking cold in the head and that's the worst of it. It always settles in a weak place when I take anything.'

A sufferer summed up her condition: 'I had this funny hand and the doctor kept talking about it but I said it isn't the hand that's bothering me but I have these heads.' Her confused approach had something in common with the ailing lady who said, 'On top of my head I had a bad stummick and then I had corns on top of everything.'

'I never knew you were down till you were up' is a comment sometimes heard. So is that of the woman who lamented, 'I'm just hanging together.' This inspired the retort, 'You aren't so bad then. I'm just hanging apart.'

Discontent with medical advice was indicated by the health centre remark, 'I hope my own doctor is on the day. I don't like the other oul fella one bit. He only gives you that oul red battle. You might as well swalley water.'

An East Belfast cry from the heart ran, 'I hate them pain killers. They'll be the death of me one of these days.' Another exclamation of distress was, 'I was on my back for a whole week for it was teemin' on me when I got home and I was seepin'.'

Heard in extern in a Belfast hospital was the complaint, 'Imagine him asking me to take my clothes aff to get my throat lucked at!' Not long after it was followed by, 'My oul lad's a boyo. His kidneys give the whole house a headache.' A woman listening then said, 'I haven't been out for a week. I thought it better not to put my foot through the door until this leg of mine eased up a bit.'

Keep to the right and you'll be flying

A Dublin woman will say, 'My husban' tuk aff his tick vest and put on a tin wan.' She will speak of 'the fort' when she means 'the fourth' and refer to a 'woit Christmas'.

An Ulsterwoman will scorn such a linguistic approach yet will say of someone, 'I never like to telefoam him for he's awful hard to lift.' This has nothing whatever to do with his weight.

She will see nothing unusual about the reply given to a motorist near Newtownards who asked, 'Can you tell me where this road leads to?' and was told, 'Och many a time a knowed but a dinnae half know aught noo.'

This was in direct contrast to the advice given another motorist who asked if he was right for Aldergrove airport. He was informed, 'Keep on to the right and you'll be flyin'.'

A census official helping a householder fill in her form asked, 'How many males have you in the house?' He was told, 'Well, we have wir breakfast, then we have wir dinner, then wir tea, and when its time to lie down a drap of cocoa. Many a night we would put on the pan before we go to bed and I'd sleep like Red Riding Hood's Aunt Peggy.'

If an Ulsterwoman describes anyone as 'good livin'' a compliment is not necessarily intended. What is conveyed is that the person referred to is intolerant of anyone who is not a devout churchgoer, who takes a drink and who is guilty at times of intemperate language. He or she will have

41

'Keep on to the right and you'll be flyin'.'

a close knowledge of the Scriptures, and be able to recite John 3.16, word for word, at the drop of a hat.

Reluctance to go for an evening walk will be shown by the statement, 'It's awful bad round here at night. Even John Wayne wouldn't go out after dark.'

In her early fifties a lady would consider she had been mortally insulted by the new postman, uncertain of the address on a letter, who called to her from the other side of the street in tones all could hear, 'Are you 58?'

The same lady would be liable, when admiring a friend's baby, to ask the infant's age and when told 'eighteen months' inquire, 'What do you call him?' Told 'It's Nathan', she would exclaim in surprise, 'But surely you have given the child a name by now?'

She would warn a visitor, 'Mind where you sit. The wee lad sticks his gubbly bum everywhere.' And say of her husband, 'He's got a nice wee job with a removal firm. Now he's carrying all before him.' She is apt to grumble, 'That wee girl of ours is a desperate child. The hiss of her hair spray would deafen you.'

It would be completely in character for her to say of a friend 'She's a fine big woman and stout with it.' And, after pushing her way to the last seat in a bus, to tell the driver, 'Ave been waitin' at that stap for the last half hour. That fella drivin' the bus in front of you went by with the sture flyin' from his back wheels. I put my haun out to him but he wènt past like the hammers and just lef' me stannin' there like a stewed prune.'

I'd know that bake of hers anywhere

Oscar Wilde once said of George Bernard Shaw, 'He hasn't an enemy in the world and none of his friends like him.' There is much the same flavour about the Ulsterwoman's comment on politicians, 'Some of them aren't bad but none of them's any use.' Nor is it likely that the lady was a mine of information about the observations of Wilde.

Philosophical comments take many forms in the Province. 'I was just going away in to get on me only I thought it wouldn't matter what I wore and what's on me would pass me.' Much more explicit is, 'I haven't seen her for years but I'd know that oul bake of hers anywhere.'

Resolve was displayed by a County Armagh woman who had left her native town to live in Belfast. She took ill and told a friend who visited her in hospital, 'If anything happens to me it would break my heart to think I'd be buried in Belfast. If I live till I die I'll be buried in Tynan, should I have to walk it.'

A lady with a son who was all of six and a half feet tall looked proudly up at him and told a visitor, 'Right enough he's tall but sure he was tall since he was no size.' The way another woman put it was, 'I couldn't believe how my grandson had grown. 'Clare to me God, when he walked through the door the other day there I thought he had grown another head.'

There was nothing equivocal about the statement of the

mother who told a friend, 'If they ask me if I mind wee Willie being slapped at school I'll tell them they can bate the livin' daylights outa him, the wee divil.'

Traffic hazards were summed up by a Belfastwoman in a style of her own: 'A day like that, if you stepped out on the road you'd be knocked down and killed stone dead and there'd be two more cars over you before you'd have time to get up.'

A desire to avoid a direct statement is not uncommon. A shopkeeper who was asked how business was doing said, 'Some days there'll be quite a few customers but other days there's not so many.' When the questioner persisted by asking what was the average she replied, 'The average varies a lot.'

The woman who remarked, 'I've noticed something different about Jimmy since he lost his leg', was, perhaps, showing a sharp sense of observation, but an understandable awareness was reflected by the security man, happy at his work, who told a colleague, 'The clock's goin' roun' rightly the night.'

From Derry, severely hit by unemployment, came the profound comment, 'Sure if you manage to get your hands on a good, steady job your bread's baked for life.' And there is finality about the words of the woman whose husband bought her a second-hand typewriter he said had been 'a quare bargain': 'That's a stupid thing to get me. A typewriter! Man dear it's about as useful as a back pocket in a duncher.'

The same practical approach was laid bare by the woman bound for Spain who was asked by a passport office official, 'Do you want a one-year or a ten-year passport?' Indignantly she replied, 'What are you talking about? Sure we're only goin' for a fortnight.'

He can fairly handle his feet

Belfast is said to have more shoe shops per head of the population than any other city in the UK. Certainly footwear—women's to a greater degree than men's—is a continual preoccupation, whether for the reason that women like to know where they stand, or want to make it clear they don't have feet of clay.

A shoe shop assistant will take it in his stride when confronted by a customer who says, 'I'm looking for a half decent pair of shoes for walking for I can't get my feet off my mind.'

And reflecting the concern at getting about in comfort is the exchange:

'When I ran into your husband yesterday he had an awful scowl on his face. Is he sick?'

'Ach, pay no attention to our Sandy. It's them shoes he bought. They're that tight you'd think they were painted on to his feet. He bought them at the sale at half price, the ijit, and they're giving him gyp. I told him to stuff them with wet paper and leave them to soften under the bed but he keeps wearing them to break them in. I told him he'd give himself bad feet for life but I might as well talk to the wall.'

'Is that what's wrong? I thought I had tramped on his toe.'

The same trouble was probably at the source of the Shankill Road woman's lament, 'I was away down in Tullymore Forest in them shoes. They're all right for steppin' out in but damn the bit of use are they for walking.'

Objecting to the price asked for the shoes she had chosen a woman declared, 'I wouldn't pay that for them. Sure you'd have to buy a hat to show them off.'

Those who enjoy the bliss of healthy feet are a constant object of envy: 'That wee woman who lives at the corner, she doesn't know how lucky she is. She's awful light on her feet. She's seventy if she's a day and last Friday I saw her run as souple as a hare after the coal man.'

The same wistful longing was echoed in the statement, 'That fella can fairly handle his feet, so he can. He's a dab hand with them. I never saw anybody as handy with their feet as him. You'd wonder how he does it.'

It isn't only in the shoe shops that the things people say reflect their obsession with footwear:

'I'm away to get a pair of shoes for my man. I usually let him go for his own feet only between blisters and bunions the man hasn't a foot to walk on.'

'That shop I was in yesterday, I wouldn't go back there again for a pair of shoes. All they do is wipe your eye.'

'I told the assistant my left fut was away with it and she said, "I hope you shut the door."'

'Every time I catch the flu it goes to my head and takes the feet from under me.'

'This is a great pair of shoes I got. I bought them six weeks ago and I haven't had them off since.'

When she said 'Shout?' I shouted

Few days pass without a new crop of contributions to the pronunciation oddities which fill the Ulster air. They are used unsparingly, often deliberately.

A woman who told a chemist, 'I want a bottle for a caff' puzzled him and he suggested, 'Why don't you try a vet? If you have a caff with a cough it's all you can do.' 'But it's me that has the caff', she protested, and coughed to prove it.

Besides the now familiar allusions to Norn Iron there are such variations as 'Noran Auorlan'. It is an area with its own 'seeketary of Stayot' and has a 'soshull securitah systum' sometimes described by politicians as a 'toal scrace'.

Sisters can be turned into 'sosters' and brothers into 'brawers', while a parent will be described as 'the childers' forr'. Anyone heard speaking of 'weemen' is not alluding to males of small stature.

After several experiences at security checkpoints a visitor inquired, 'Why do the police get the idea that I'm called Ed? Actually a woman PC said it to me yesterday. It happens every time I'm stopped and my car is checked. When it is clear all I get is "Go Ed." It's very odd seing my name is Cyril.'

A Belfastman got into some trouble with his wife who charged him with needlessly annoying a neighbour. 'You roared your head off at the woman when she called to see

'When I answered her knock she said "Shout?" and I shouted.'

me', she accused. His explanation was accepted with marked reluctance. 'When I answered her knock she said "Shout?" and I shouted. What was wrong with that?'

A similar misunderstanding arose at a boxing tournament when a woman spectator spotted a friend three rows ahead and asked her husband to catch his attention. 'Stan', he called. Instantly four people in the next row got to their feet.

If a woman tells you firmly, 'There's no glypes in Ire Street', she is seeking to stress that her neighbours are the salt of the earth and that the residents of her street are solid citizens to a man.

From childhood the urge to put things differently is in evidence. A teacher was having trouble persuading her class to pronounce the word 'hammer' in the proper way. Some said 'hamma', others 'ammar'. She picked out one offender and told him, 'Say ham.' He did so. 'Now say mare', she directed and he obeyed. 'Now what is it?' she asked. After a moment's thought the boy replied, 'It's a thing you howl in ye haun for luckin' at yerself.'

An Ulsterwoman walking along a Hong Kong street stopped to look in a shop window and found that her husband had gone ahead. Anxious not to lose him in the crowd she called out, 'Howl on.' Three Chinese immediately stopped and one asked her, 'What is it you want?' She then made the chastening discovery that Howl On is a common Chinese name.

A milkman was asked how he came to nickname one of his runs 'Chinatown'. 'Time after time when I call at a house to get a bill paid,' he explained, 'a youngster will come to the door and say "Shintin."'

It was different in another area he served where a woman was heard grumbling, 'You hafta be up early to catch our milkman', as if he were a kind of prey.

Is them roses for down your back?

Women in Ulster may not be the world's best dressed but this is not to say they lack clothes sense; far from it. A chat between two bus passengers sums up their attitude:

'Doesn't a lovely day like that make you think of something new to wear? I set out to get myself a complete new rig-out when I thought to myself, what's the use? Sez I to myself, there's no sense buying one just to hang in the wardrobe, although mind you I like to have one in the wardrobe. Just in case.'

'You're right, Martha. You need a rig-out in the wardrobe to fall back on. Where are you if you haven't got one? That's what I always say.'

Concern is constantly voiced when it comes to the way the man of the house will look. One woman said of him, 'He was all cut because I didn't pack his simmit. He said his holiday was buggered.' Wifely concern was also shown by, 'Even if I say it myself, they were the best pair of trousers he ever had on his back.'

Callers have a nasty habit of arriving at the wrong time. One was told, 'Howl on a wee minute. I won't be a tick till I put on myself and I'll be down.' This probably indicated that it was planned to change from the skin out.

Children's clothes are never quite right. One complaint ran, 'I don't like the way young Sammy's corduroys whostle and the way Rachel's behine moves when she walks. You'd think she was chewin' carmels.'

51

After a Lord Mayor's Show a spectator made the unexpected comment about the robes of the civic dignatories, 'Didn't the councillors look awful well in their working clothes?'

Women's hats belong to a world of their own: 'I see yer woman has that hat of hers on again. It was a right hat in its day, I'll say that. She's been wearing it a good seven years now. One of these days it'll come to bits in her hand. If it doesn't I'll swear it'll take an operation to get it off her, for she's awful attached to it.'

A new fashion note was not indicated at a garden centre when a woman asked an acquaintance, 'Is them roses you're buying for down your back? They're quaren nice. I often say about my own back that it could do with a wee bit more colour.'

A wrong impression was certainly created by the woman who told a neighbour, 'I made up my mind. I just thought I'd stick to my old clothes line.'

The teacher who couldn't spell

'Geeus a suck of yir orange and I'll show ye my beelin' heel' is a youthful invitation not unknown in Ulster. The speaker is a type whose mother would say of him, 'That wee lad has a quare head on him, so he has.'

At a County Down school a teacher calling the roll found that the absentees included the twin brother of a member of the class. She asked him if his brother was coming to school and the boy replied, 'He should be, miss, for he was washed last night.'

One youngster who answered a knock at the door called to his mother, 'There's a man givin' out tracks. He wants to know if you've saw the light.' Back came the instruction, 'Tell him to go away for we're not so bad since the man put in the wee back winda.'

At another school the children had been asked to write an essay on boats and were offered help with their spelling. One child put up his hand and asked, 'How do you spell howl, like in the howl of a boat?' The teacher wrote, 'Hold', on the blackboard. On his way home the boy was asked by a companion what he thought of the teacher. It was her first week at the school. 'She's all right,' the boy said, 'but she can't spell.'

One mother was heard to complain of her small son, 'He came home ringin' so he did. That was bad enough but only the night before he came home seepin'.'

An estimate of the younger generation ran, 'The childer nowadays wudden giv' ye a sate in the bus if ye were on crutches. Sure they think if you're able to walk you're able to stan'.'

A woman in a Belfast health centre who had a sickly-looking youngster at her side revealed all to the man beside her. 'See this wee lad here?' she said. 'He's goin' like snow aff a ditch. There isn't a pick on him, an' yet he ates like a horse. Ate ye outa house an' home, so he would, yet there's not as much fat on him as would oil a pair of spec hinges. Mind ye, the dacter tole me not to worry my head for it's the fatties that bother him, he said. When I'm at it I want to see him about these pains. Thon oul lad of mine doesn't give me much sympathy. All he says is I should be able to see the sky without luckin' up.'

Words open to misunderstanding were used by a woman in a Belfast supermarket who was trying to drag away her small son from a tempting display of sweets: 'You're too late to be luckin' now, child. I've already bought ye.'

Naturally it was a Ballymena youngster who was being questioned at Sunday school about a Scriptural passage which included the words 'Seek ye the Lord.' He was asked what 'seek' meant and promptly replied, 'It's the way you are when you're no feelin' well.'

Two small boys were arguing in a Newtownards bus. They had disagreed whether or not a woman seated in front of the vehicle was a new teacher. One said, 'Sur.' His friend said, 'Snat hur.' The first boy insisted 'Tissur', and then added firmly, 'Akit tiz thoul doll. My man says she's goin' till learn us English.'

There is a strong possibility that his mother could be credited with the note sent to school which read, 'Please excuse Johnny's lessons as he was sick at the weak end.' His plight had certain similarities with the boy of whom it was bluntly said, 'He has took bad.'

54

Poison
in her cistern

A sharp ear is needed to spot what's amiss with statements like, 'The doctor told me I would be all right once I got the poison out of my cistern', and, 'There's a bline man comin' to see our venetians.' Each typifies the Ulster approach to the art of failing to get it quite right. Northern Ireland has many of the qualities of a malaproprian jungle.

The mother of a bride-to-be will complain, 'We're having awful bother with her torso', and it will be said of a new pastor, 'He's very effluent.' You will be informed, 'I can say without fear of contraception that I'll be there', and to be described as an 'extemporary speaker' does not mean you are just a stand-in. The wife of an enthusiastic angler who miraculously managed to make the shore after being caught by a storm in the middle of a lake insisted that he told her he was on his own against the elephants.

Encompassing a blundering approach to the rules of grammar, as well as to logic is the statement, 'Them liquid deterrents are great. It's marvellous what you can get out of the bottles when they're empty.'

Ill-health is to blame for much verbal chaos, as in, 'The doctor put me on to female baritone tablets', 'He takes compositors for his piles', 'They sent me to hospital for tests and said I was diabolic', and 'My man's in subtraction since he broke his leg.'

There are cases where medical care has taken the form of

'The doctor told me I would be all right once I got the poison out of my cistern.'

'injunctions', and where a child has been given 'a dose of castrol oil'. It is even possible to be like the woman who said, 'I couldn't close an eye all night because I had cartridge trouble in my leg which I had to get off for a week.'

Doctors, however, can sometimes err. A patient complained, 'He said he would give me surgical stockings for my ferocious veins but they were only alastik.'

Unusual enterprise was shown by the housewife who 'got some jam jars and washed them in the jaw box to make damsel jam'. Doubtless she was the type who was 'dead keen on hysterical novels'.

A talent for the wrong word can be acquired early. This was proved by the little girl who said, 'We learned all about the Jews and the reptiles at Sunday school.'

After a trip to Switzerland a holidaymaker spoke of the enjoyment of 'a ride in one of them vernacular railways'. It is possible that her delight was only equalled by a visit to see the 'Blackpool eliminations'.

While Ulster may have its share of fatalists this is not to say that it is coming down with stamp collectors.

It is popular at New Year to go to Scotland 'for mahogany', but this did not apply to the lady whose display of washing led her next-door neighbour to comment, 'Lookin' at that line of clothes you'd think she was incontinent.' This brought the reply, 'Oh no, she's at home. I saw her this mornin'.'

You could drink her bath water

Most Ulster housewives look on their doorstep as a plat-
form on which they can speak their mind, a place for a cosy
chat with a neighbour with few subjects barred. An observation like, 'See her in twenty-nine? You could drink her
bath water so you could', has the candour of, 'See her
across the street? That woman's head's full of sweetie
mice.'

Proximity is not always considered a blessing. 'We have
the best of neighbours. We never see them from morn till
night, from one year's end to the other.' Not everyone would
hold such a view. 'I haven't a word to say against her myself,' can imply as great a dislike as, 'I wouldn't trust her
even if she was throwing stones at me.'

'When I asked that new woman two doors up if she had
any milk bottles she said she had buckets and I told her I
wasn't lookin' for any buckets', is an off-the cuff comment
liable to start off an exchange of views lasting from twenty
minutes to an hour. Much, of course, would depend on the
weather.

It is always possible for an encounter to consist of mono-
logues, each contribution completely independent of the
other:

'That fella Cissie M'Clurg's gettin' married to—he has a
face like a well-kept grave and that's the God's truth.'

'There's nathan to bate a coal fire for warmin' yir back-
side, my man always says.'

'There's this about Jimmy down the street. You couldn't have met better before he fell into the drink.'

'It's a pity about Mrs Darty up the street. Her man never left her a mortal hate in his will.'

'I took our wee Hughey to Donaghadee in the bus yesterday and when I put him into the water he hung on to me like a limpet.'

'The man in forty-seven told me he drives a mail lorry and I asked him if he worked for the Post Office. "No" he says, "it's a pig mail lorry." I didn't know he was from Cullybackey.'

The longer the street the greater the reliance on the numbers of their houses rather than the names of people being talked about. 'That girl in forty-nine—I put myself out to stay in for her so I did. I might as well not have bothered my head.'

Many women would be at a loss without a neighbour in whom to confide, to favour with such admissions as:

'I go to Bingo to take me away from myself.'

'I've nearly finished the Mills and Boon I got in the library. Them books is the quare mark.'

'My oul granny had the time of it in them days when you could go into a shop and tell them, "A packet of Woodbines and write it down as a wee loaf."'

'That new BBC announcer—you couldn't keep from listening to him even if he says nothing.'

A neighbourly chat also offers an opportunity to pass on a piece of advice. 'I always leave the skin on a cucumber for there's nothing like it for cutting the wind.'

But neighbours can have their drawbacks. 'The woman next door is a terrible one for borrowing. Know what I'm going to tell you? I was in her house the other day and when I looked round me I felt far more at home in her kitchen than I did in my own.'

The hat water's up the pole

When on holiday in Rome an Ulsterwoman saw a banknote lying on the pavement. As she bent to pick it up a voice behind her was heard exclaiming, 'If luck's on the road I'm in the sheugh.' Not another word was needed to establish that the comment came from another Northern Ireland visitor.

Nor would the Benidorm hotel receptionist have been in any doubt about the nationality of the caller on the house phone who said, 'Hi there. I'm Shooey's wife up here in savan thee thee. Lissen. The classit's clogged, the shire's bust, the sunpline's on the plink, and the hat water's up the pole. Wud ye send up yer man?'

If it is suggested that Ulster people abroad stick out like a sore thumb this does them an injustice. The same applies to Geordies, those who speak Scouse, or people from Cork. One possible distinction is that those from Northern Ireland tend to regard as stupid anyone who fails to understand them. A Civil Guard will be stopped in Magaluf and told, 'My hambeg's neucked', and the speaker will make it clear that if he doesn't instantly appreciate that her handbag has been stolen the man is brainless.

In Estoril two attractive girls lay stretched out on the beach in the hot sun. Some fifteen or twenty yards behind were two young men who kept tossing pebbles at them. Finally one of the girls raised herself and shouted, 'Wud yousens nack aff the cloddin and give people a bitta peace?' As the youths darted off an Ulster holidaymaker nearby said approvingly, 'You didden half tell themmuns aff.' One of the girls replied, 'Aye I saw they got the quare gunk when Mary here lost the bap.' It is probable that a lack of understanding of the exchanges was not only lost on any French, German or Spanish ears. English listeners would have been no less confused.

A difficulty of another variation arose when a County Antrim couple were having trouble with the menu in a Spanish restaurant and a waiter stepped over to help. 'We are so sorry', he explained. 'The ham is not. The chicken has not been either. But the eggs you can have tight or loose.' Although completely in the dark they said, 'Well then, we'll have them loose.' Before long they were enjoying scrambled eggs on toast.

It took a little time for a Majorcan shopkeeper to realise what was being sought when told, 'I want a sun hat to sit on my back', and a Civil Guard in Benalmedena needed time to appease the visitor who complained to him, 'They tole us this place was stikkin' out. Stikkin' out me fut.'

A Belfastwoman, highly conscious that she was a stranger in a strange land, found herself in the midst of a group in Berlin gathered round a pet shop from which a small reptile had got loose. The suggestions, in German, about how to get it back came thick and fast. Any homesickness the woman may have felt was dispelled when she heard a shout from behind her: 'Hit the windy a skelp and mebbe it'll lep back in again.'

There is every chance that an Ulster party filled the bus in which the comment was heard: 'What I didn't like about them high rize apartments is that if you walk in your sleep it's good-night.' Overheard in the same bus was the tell-tale remark: 'The man gave us a free battle of wine. The next morning he ast did it do any damage. I tole him it was powerful. It nearly took the roof aff.'

Have ye
annie lemmuns?

During the sales a Belfast store supervisor was approached by an indignant shopper who demanded: 'What's this place coming to? If I'd known I wouldn't have brought my wee girl along with me.' The bewildered man, full of apologies, wanted to know what was wrong. 'They said on the loud speaker there was a nudist play on this floor', she said angrily. 'Where is it?' The lady was not at all happy when it was pointed out that there was nothing more than a new display of furniture.

Shopkeepers receive so many odd requests that they must all be incapable of being surprised. 'I want a small fish tank for a child' is a demand they can take in their stride. It won't make them think of calling the NSPCC. They know not to show surprise when asked for 'a lawn-mower that cuts grass', or they hear a mother, when buying a sweater for her small son, tell him: 'Throw it over your head.'

A newly arrived supervisor from England on duty in a British Home Store in Belfast ran into difficulties when faced with a woman who asked, 'Have ye annie lemmuns?' He blinked at the lady and said, 'I'm sorry, madam. I don't quite understand.' She gave him an indignant look and, in a voice for the entire store to hear, demanded: 'Jezus, do they nat know English in this hole no more?'

In one store a request ran: 'I'm looking for a tie for my

husband. Not very bright.' A shopper with a dog on a lead told an assistant 'I want a ball for this bloody dog.'

A woman seeking a packet of sticks was asked if she wanted one at 10p or 20p. 'I'm not a bit particular', she replied. 'They're only for lightin' the fire.' The lady who said she wanted to see the assistant who 'walks with a slight lips' eventually found satisfaction, as did the shopper who insisted, 'It isn't a sweater I need, it's a jumper.'

In a Londonderry store the following cry of distress was heard: 'I've spent pounds the day and I haven't a parcel you could plug your ears with.'

A customer who was dissatisfied with a box of chocolates she bought as a Christmas present declared, 'They're terrible.' She was promptly advised, 'Then why don't you give them to somebody you don't like.' Another, in some doubt about a jacket she wanted for her small son, commented: 'The wee lad's big of himself.' This inspired the advice, 'I know, but he'll grow into it.'

In one small country shop a woman wanted to pay for an article she had got on credit but was unable to remember what exactly it was. The shopkeeper said, 'I can't remember either, Mrs Kendy, but sure you can pay for it when it comes into your head.' A woman standing nearby broke in: 'Sure I was here when she got it. It was a packet of tea. She got half a dozen cracked eggs, a box of matches, a tube of toothpaste, a toilet roll, half a pound of raisins, a packet of sugar, a battle of Ferry Lickwood, a packet of cornflakes, and a bar of Cadbury's milk, and didn't have enough in her purse.' Then she added, 'There was a wee plump woman who bought a sedlitz poweder and a battle of aspirins. She was stannin' beside her.'

That bacon, Aggie. It skites.

Visitors to Northern Ireland are to be pitied for missing out on the crack when travelling in a crowded country bus. The richness of the comment about a redundant husband would be lost on them: 'Ach all he does now is the odd bit of gardenin'. He dotes on lettuces. He says they break the mahogany.'

The same would apply to the remarks of a woman who was describing a search for carpets. 'I liked the look of the cord backed ones the man showed me. It would be grand at the price, I said to myself, but I knew that when it gets wet it's curtains.'

'I need a new map. My oul head's done. I have it a long time', would be Greek to a stranger as would the comment, 'He's a man who always goes to his charch.' Similarly there would be difficulty in appreciating the remark, 'Maggie has started going to her place of worship. I knew it would surprise you to hear but she promised her mother she would. Anyway it shouldn't do her all that much harm.'

'I met Madge at big John's funeral', was one revelation. 'She was bent over his coffin muttering away there, saying, 'He's awful like himself. I mind the day he was born'.'

Chatting in a shopping queue a woman told her companion, 'That man of mine would give a saint the nyrps. Me, I just gave him the rounds of the kitchen.' This brought the reply, 'Me? I just tole mine aff.'

Few English milkmen would know what was meant by

'When he came back from the feel the hum of his feet was
desperate.'

the note left for one in Armagh: 'Put a bottle behine the door an' pull till.' Only in an Ulster supermarket would anyone understand the advice 'Don't take that bacon, Aggie It skites.'

Another instruction which went rather astray was given to a breadserver. It happened when a husband was asked to leave a note saying that no bread would be needed that day. Obediently he wrote, 'Please leave NO! bread today thanks.' That evening two loaves were found on the windowsill accompanied by a missive which read 'I don't know what you mean by No. 1 bread so I have left you the best I have.'

The husband who brings home a photograph of himself and finds his wife full of enthusiasm about it can count himself fortunate. The average reaction is that shown by a Newtownards woman who said of her husband's driving licence picture 'My God, Jimmy, you look like a layin' hen that hada coul haun stuck under it.'

The wife who had to be up at an early hour to get her husband off to work summed up her feelings with the comment, 'When I looked out at six o'clock this morning the air would have peeled the paint off the last post.'

It is not unlike the remark of the lady whose husband had taken part in the ten-mile Twelfth of July Orange parade to the customary venue, a large field: 'When he came back from the feel the hum of his feet was desperate.'

There is the same air of dismissiveness about the way a County Fermanagh farmer's wife assessed the new hand: 'By the cut of that fella's jib a pair of boots is going to last him a long time.'

Is that day going to do?

A comment on the weather, be it 'Nice day', 'Bit wet', or 'Looks promising', can have special significance. The tone used is an important indicator of the speaker's opinion of the person to whom the remark is made.

If it is someone considered a mortal enemy there will be a curt nod, which barely acknowledges their existence. The comment 'Quite cool' can be like an accusation that the woman addressed was entirely to blame for the fact. If a close friend it will be 'Lovely day, Sarah' or 'Nothing wrong with that morning, eh?' If it is someone of whom the speaker is not quite sure a casual 'Warm' or 'Wettish' will be uttered.

While conversation about the weather is laden with such undertones, in most cases a perfectly friendly relationship is reflected. 'Do you think that day's going to do?' is a question put by one acknowledged expert in weather lore to another, from one whose judgment is usually respected to one whose status is acknowledged. This contrasts with the down to earth attitude of the woman who said to her next door neighbour, 'It looks nice so long as you're in but when you're out you'd think your fingers were going to fall off. Then you wish you were in again.' Equally unpleasant conditions gave rise to, 'I looked out this morning and it was pouring down my back like a solid waterfall.'

Ulster's damp climate naturally means that references to wet conditions are the most frequent:

'She said she was ringin' an' the funny thing is her name's Bell.'

'Children would break your heart. They came home from school yesterday with the water drippin' outa them in quarts.'

A woman standing at a bus stop said, 'That rain's desperate. It's the wettest I've ever felt. Do you think it will keep up?' 'Not the way it's comin' down anyway,' was the reply.

Severe weather is frequently an accompaniment to other misfortunes, as was the case with the Dungannon resident who had this to say: 'With my oul father lyin' up in his bed with one fut in the grave an' the other slidin' in, I don't know whether I'm comin' or goin'. My husband there, sittin' naggin' about the cramps in his inside, thinks he has a gnat in his puddin', and poor wee Tommy needin' a physic because he's all dried up. It's enough to drive anybody roun' the ben'. An' if that wasn't enough luck at the oul rain. It isn't even takin' time to come down on ye.' The inference is clear that if it had only been dry her travail wouldn't have been half as bad.

I'm just livin' on suction

Teeth run feet a close second when it comes to middle-aged obsessions in Ulster, and dentures are always a popular conversation topic. When asked how she was managing since she had all her teeth extracted a Limavady woman answered, 'To tell you the God's truth I'm just livin' on suction.'

A Belfast milkman seeking payment of his bill was told, 'I can't pay this week for I have no teeth in.' A Cullybackey woman explained to a friend: 'I got four teeth out and my man came with me for company. Sammy's awful thoughtful. I didn't feel a thing, sure I didn't, Sammy?'

In a Comber bus a woman was heard telling her companion, 'When I said the child had a dirty nappy she said it was probably only from her teeth.'

This comment about a dentist cannot be called entirely typical: 'That man makes me sick. When he was drillin' he kep' tellin' me to keep my mouth shut. What did he expec'? Anyway a dentist isn't like anybody else. He'll say to you wud you take a drink and then ask you to spit it out.'

In a County Armagh Post Office the assistant was asked by a pensioner, 'I wonder if you'd mind lickin' them stamps for me for I've no teeth in?' Tartly she replied, 'Woman dear, you only lick them. You don't ate them.'

The new dentures of a Dungannon woman were causing her some trouble and she told her husband, 'I'm going to keep my teeth in tonight.' 'Well, if you're not going to take them out you might as well just keep them in,' he said helpfully.

Conversation in a dentist's waiting room can be as revealing as that in a doctor's surgery. 'The things they tell you when they get you in that chair. I mind one fella who said if I didn't chew the reg so much I'd have better teeth. I told him I was there to get my teeth pulled, nat my leg.'

Another exchange concerned dentures on holidays and led to the revelation, 'When I go away I always take a sperr perr now, for the last time I was in Malta I lost my best ones when I was in the water. Niver saw hilt nor hare of them again. I can't tell you what it did to our holiday. I kept biting my man's nose aff.' 'Right enough you must have had some teething troubles,' was the sympathetic response.

A patient who said she was having so much trouble with her plaque that she was 'plaque and blue' commented, 'A woman I know went to get a tooth out in Cyprus and you should have seen her. The man made a right hand of her mouth.' A lady alongside added: 'Ever since my husband got his teeth out he keeps saying fangs aren't what they used to be. I can't help feeling sorry for him all the same. All he finds heartening now is champ.'

They served the drink in plastic glasses

Most Ulsterwomen have long ceased to expect their admirers to sweep them off their feet. Impulsive sweethearts are not easily come by and there are many stories emphasising the reticence which comes before a proposal of marriage and the extreme caution where final committal is involved.

Is the fault with the ladies? Take the County Down farmer who was driving past the village graveyard with the object of his desire. He laid his cards on the table by exclaiming, 'Mary, how would you like to be buried with our ones?' And the venerable admirer who took the plunge by suggesting, 'Maggie, what would you say to the pair of us keeping our teeth in the one mug?' Another wooer who tried the same tack said, 'Lizzie, wouldn't your washin' be a deal more homely lookin' with a shirt or two on the same line?'

The presumption is that in each case there was an eager assent but could it be that there have been exceptions and the response was an acid 'Man, but you're the silly oul ijit' or, 'My God, man, don't you come out with the right rubbish?'

Is it possible that male wariness is largely based on an anxiety to avoid a biting answer? What man likes to be put in his place? Take the tentative admirer who kept a regular twice-a-week rendezvous underneath a massive oak tree at a crossroads with the lady of whom he had a notion:

'Mary, how would you like to be buried with our ones?'

'Agnes, I have something to tell you.'

'What would that be?'

We won't be meeting here much longer.'

'You mean we're going to get married?' she asked uncertainly.

'Ach, Agnes, don't be ridiculous. They're going to cut this tree down and build a couple of houses here. We'll just have to meet somewhere else.'

Women are so rarely lost for words that it is impossible to think she didn't instantly give him the rough edge of her tongue.

A triumph in the matrimonial stakes can often bring sharp comment:

'Did you hear about Mary Jane? She's gone and got married and her poor oul man hardly settled in his grave?'

'I know. I heard that. But sure the woman never had an ounce. I'm told they had a poor wedding anyway. Did you know they served the drink in plastic glasses?'

The same reaction is echoed in, 'Did you hear that William John is going to marry that one from the other end of the town?'

'Away to hell! Sure she's as oul as the hills, that one. Nivver aff the gallop to the doctor's.'

There is nothing unusual about the philosophy reflected in the rebuke of a mother to the teacher who complained of her daughter's poor school attendance. 'Our Eleanor was never great at the learnin', and she got a man. Our Ruth wasn't much use at it either and she got a man. Him and her want for nothin'. So if you think I'm going to lose a night's sleep because wee Annie's a bit behine in her lessons you have another think comin'.'

If a young woman says of a suitor 'He's all right', it should not be assumed that he is regarded with approval. The words can be as dismissive as 'I wouldn't warm to that character even if he was covered in HP sauce.'

I could ate a whole loaf without opening it

Most Ulsterwomen firmly believe in calling a spade a spade. When interviewed on a radio programme a woman was asked, 'What are you doing at this moment?' She replied, 'I'm speaking on the wireless.' During a discussion on slimming a Larne housewife said, 'I don't believe in starving myself. My ma always said if you don't widen you weezin.'

After a long absence the patron of a Belfast café inquired if the venerable waitress, still serving, had ever married. When told she was still single he said, 'My God, the woman's going to die wondering.'

A Dundonald woman, challenged with the inquiry 'Where did I see your face before?' retorted, 'The same place as you see it now.'

The doctor who put the question to a patient, 'What's your trouble?' was promptly told, 'A pain in the neck but I don't think you could do a thing about him.'

A despairing shopper lamented to her friend, 'The prices these days keep going up and up that much that I feel like going home and cuttin' my throat.' This brought the response, 'Not a bad idea at all, Gillian. If you do, be sure and come roun' and do mine when you're at it.'

Boastfulness is usually given short shrift. The claims of a long distance yachtsman were dismissed with the comment, 'Him! I've rung more salt water out of our George's socks than he ever sailed in.'

74

Opticians were put in their place by the Ballymena woman who was heard to assess them thus: 'Apticians! They're the boys. Them fellas wud put specs on a donkey if it let them.'

A girl boarding a long-distance Ulsterbus was asked if she would like two smoking seats. She replied, 'I'm not a bit fussy so long as they don't go on fire.'

In a supermarket the mother of a small boy who was helping himself at a confectionery display rebuked him. 'Put them sweeties back this minute. They're not for atin'. I just need some for meers for we're flyin' off to Spain the marra.'

An urgent need for a meal was signalled by, 'I'm starvin'. I could ate a whole loaf without openin' it.' And there was an element of logic in the advice, 'The woman you're after lives next door. But you'll have to give it a right dunder for she's awful hard of hearing. One of these days she'll have no door left with people hammerin' it in.'

Difficulties in finding someone eager and willing to do a small house-repair job were crystallised by the indictment, 'This place is comin' down with O-aye men. You tell them the water's pourin' down the kitchen walls and they say, "O-aye." You tell them the spoutin's leakin' like Niagara Falls and they say, "O-aye." You say to the man in the garage that the car's leakin' oil by the bucketful and what do you get? "O-aye." Wudden it sicken ye?'

She'd ate the arm off Moses

Eating out is as much a family event in Ulster as in any other part of the world. Carry-out facilities have had their effect, as has the chippy, but neither has taken over entirely.

Tradition dies hard. A family of six had seated themselves round a café table, full of expectancy, and the mother reached for the menu. Before she had time to start a study of the gastronomic delights which might be in store her husband, a man with a one-track mind, announced decisively, 'Ni for a good fry.'

Waitresses take the oddest requests in their stride. It is part of the job to avoid raising an eyebrow at the statement, 'I don't think I'll bother with a sweet. I'll just have a wee bit of cheese to taste my mouth.'

One complaint took an unusual form: 'Them coffee calculators make the coffee taste awful funny.'

The absence of a member of a family at a table was simply explained: 'I had to leave the wee lad at home for he has a beelin' heel, a cowpy stummick, a sore nose, and can't look outa his eyes. Anyway people only stare when he starts vamitin'.'

The inability to do justice to a well-prepared meal was revealed by, 'I'll not want much for my guts is gone to hell. No big helpin's.'

In a County Armagh restaurant where two families were sharing a table a member of the party commented, 'That

'Take her out and she'd ate the arm off Moses.'

wee girl of your's is desprit peaky lookin'. Isn't she atin?' There was no hesitation about the reply. 'Atin? See her? Take her out and she'd ate the arm off Moses.'

A husband who showed considerable annoyance about his bill was warned sternly, 'All you can do, Brendan, is pay up and look pleasant. If you start tryin' your hand at gettin' away without puttin' your hand in your pocket you'll be needin' the quare good bannister.'

A notice in a Belfast restaurant which provides chairs for those who can't find a table during the rush hour displays a notice, 'Please wait to be seated.' It is one way of suggesting that prospective diners should hold their horses rather than rush around in search of a vacant place.

Conversation during meals inevitably produces its gems. 'My feet's twice the size trampin' roun' the shaps. You should have seen some of the coats they're sellin' at the sales, Martha. You wouldn't have went to the toilet in them.'

A comment overheard in a North Antrim restaurant, 'He took awful bad and his wife cooked him till the minute he died', would startle most hearers but only if they were unaware that in this district 'cooked' simply means 'nursed'.

I just couldn't place her

The suggestion was once made to me that the only way to render the Ulster dialect less bewildering to strangers is to view it with the distaste it merits and stop using it. Then it was added, 'It is unspeakable that such a blatant abuse of the English language has been allowed to continue for so long. That those who profess to love Ulster can be actually proud of such a travesty emphasises only their own complacent coarseness. Wilful abuse of the English language, a gift of the roots of which most of us are so supposedly proud, should be stamped out at an early age if we are not to remain a laughing stock for ever, however forlorn a hope that may be.'

I do not consider my role to be that of a latter day Fowler, handing out authoritative rulings on sloppy grammar and pronunciation oddities. The utterances I record are to be heard day and daily. They are not invented. The fact remains that those to whom they were addressed comprehended their meaning. The woman who said, 'I knew her but I just couldn't place her', and her friend who explained, 'Half my back is in tarmac and the rest is in concrete but I'm going to make it all the same when the weather improves', are completely understood. Thus I put myself firmly on the side of free speech. Without it life would be much more drab.

If the purists had their way we would outlaw such assertions as, 'He drove with too much drink.' Everyone in Ulster would be perfectly well aware that this did not imply the commital of a traffic offence because the vehicle was overloaded.

Rigid syntax would impose a need for a rephrasing order on the man who declared, 'The cross channel ferry lets you drive a car over the water', and on the claim, 'See them tyres on that car? It's what I never had to put into them was wine.'

Stamping out erroneous usages at an early age would bring condemnation on the boy who rolled a car wheel into a garage and told the attendant, 'My da says could you give this tyre a wee jeg.'

'When I got home last night there was your man hanging on to the knocker', would presumably be an offence as punishable as culpable homicide, as would the exchange, 'What time is it? Is it seven yet?' The young man who had been asked the question looked at his watch and said, 'It's just five and twenty-two.' 'I'm asking you a simple question', came the retort. 'Is it before seven or after it? Don't you bloody know, man?'

The volunteer at a blood transfusion centre who, having provided his contribution, asked the nurse, 'Can you go for a pint now?' and was told, 'I'm sorry but I don't finish till half-four', would be in trouble. So too would the husband employed by a man named Hughes who told his wife, 'I'm going to the bank for oul Hughes in the morning', when she demanded, 'Couldn't he go for his own shoes?'

Frankly, I have to say I plump for free speech.